The Long, L-o-n-g-e-r, *L-o-n-g-e-s-t* Day

By Billie Hicklin

Copyright © 2020 Billie Hicklin

All rights reserved

ISBN 978-0-578-71360-1

Dedication

This book is written with love for all of the students, staff, parents, and community members who were "the helpers" on 'The Longest Day' at Parkway School.

The event happened 25 years ago and is still discussed, related to new staff members, told to each new class of students, and referred to on any day when the weather looks threatening.

May we all continue to bring out the best in one another in times of need. Here's to Parkway in its "Finest Hour.*"

*This phrase was used by Principal Gary Childers to describe the admirable actions of the Parkway School community on January 26, 1996. It is taken from the Winston Churchill speech: "Let us therefore brace ourselves to our duties, and so bear ourselves that, if the British Empire and its Commonwealth (Parkway School) last for a thousand years, men will still say: 'This was their finest hour.'"

Foreword

Parkway School is located about six miles east of Boone, North Carolina. As indicated by the name, it is positioned on US Highway 421, parallel to the Blue Ridge Parkway. The driveway is directly across from the Parkway's Grand View Overlook, where thousands of tourists stop to take in the panoramic beauty of the Blue Ridge Mountains. The school is part of Watauga County near the community of Deep Gap, named so because of the gaps between the mountains. When it is clear in the rest of Watauga County, fog can fill the valleys and make it impossible to see very far. Road signs announce "Fog Likely" as drivers enter the area. A blinking light at the driveway to the school is the only way a driver knows where to turn into the school on extremely foggy days. Cold air often sinks into these gaps during the winter months, causing freezing rain or sleet to coat surfaces. When the northern and western parts of the county get snowfall, the eastern part often experiences the effects of icing, causing slippery, often dangerous travel conditions.

The driveway that leads to the parking lot and front of the school as well as to the bus lot in the back is a slope. Likewise this slope is an uphill climb when leaving the school to proceed onto US Highway 421. This sloping driveway was the only entrance to and exit from the school in January of 1996.

It is also important to point out that US 421 was the main road between Wilkesboro and points east and Boone, NC. All traffic had to use this highway – Appalachian State students, truckers, tourists, and local residents relied on this main artery. The Blue Ridge Parkway connected the Deep Gap area to the Blowing Rock area in southern Watauga County and beyond, but it was not treated during inclement weather in the winter and was often closed to traffic. Years later, a four-lane bypass was built around the Deep Gap Community, and US Highway 421 that paralleled the Blue Ridge Parkway became Old Highway 421. A second entrance to the school was created across from the ramp leading to the Blue Ridge Parkway.

x

Prologue

What would you do if you somehow couldn't go home from school one day? No buses, no cars, no trucks could be on the road. What would you do? Someone would have to take charge. Someone would have to keep everyone safe. Someone would have to find food for every student and staff member. Someone would have to let parents know what was happening to their children. Would you be scared? Would you cry? Would you have to do schoolwork all through the afternoon and evening? Would you have any fun in this situation? Could it be an adventure?

This story is about what happened and how the students and staff of Parkway School reacted on the day the road suddenly iced over and no one could leave. Read *The Long, Longer, Longest Day* to find out how Parkway's students and staff members worked together to answer all of these questions and more. Find out how this experience on January 26, 1996, etched a memory into the minds of everyone who experienced it, even twenty-five years later.

1.

A Normal Friday at Parkway School

January 26, 1996, started like most days at Parkway School. Teachers were arriving early in the chilly morning air to prepare for a busy Friday. Some students were being dropped off by parents at the front door, and some were arriving on buses beside the gym in the back parking lot. Greetings of "Good Morning!" rang out through the hallways as students gathered in the cafeteria to await the bell signaling the start of the day. There was more than the usual excitement because it was Friday, and students talked about their weekend plans to ski or play basketball, to sleep over with a friend, to go out of town, or go to a movie. It was a joyous sound as everyone anticipated a happy day of school with friends and adults who cared about them. Parkway was a school that felt like a family.

When the bell rang, students from Kindergarten through 8th grade scattered down the hallways to their classrooms, with teachers reminding them not to run. Loud chatter, lockers slamming shut, laughter, and teacher welcomes filled the air. As students arrived in their seats with their materials needed for the day, quiet slowly reigned throughout the building as morning business began. Announcements crackled from the intercom to signal the official start of the day. The roll was called in each class, morning work was tackled, and group time commenced on the rug in kindergarten. Basketballs bounced in the gym as the band started rehearsal and the chorus practiced in the music rooms. First graders talked about the date, the weather, and the time. Upper grade students tackled math and science problems, and reading skills were improving across every classroom. Students filed into the library for story time or to check out books. Some children practiced keyboarding skills in the computer lab and others worked with clay in art class. The cafeteria staff cleaned up from breakfast and started preparing lunch. They laughed and talked as they went about their work. The office staff answered phones and typed newsletters and met with parents and kept all the records of the busy life of Parkway School. The sights and sounds of another productive school day filled the air.

It was a gloomy day outside – gray and cloudy and too cold for outdoor recess. There was no snow or other precipitation in the forecast, though the clouds and "feel" of the air made it seem possible. As the morning routine unfolded, no one was noticing the light misty rain and falling temperatures occurring outside. As common as snow and ice were, students (and staff!) still got a thrill from either an early dismissal due to snow and especially a school cancellation, but the weather was not grabbing anyone's attention on this morning.

The rhythm of the day proceeded as usual, but just before noon the change coming in the weather was soon noted by the administrators at the central office and the leadership at all schools. Weather forecasts were consulted and it was determined that there was a strong possibility of an icing event in the county. Classes continued and the lunch schedule began. Everyone was surprised when it was announced around noon that school would dismiss early at 1:00 p.m. This created even more excitement on this Friday afternoon! Lunch was rushed along and students returned to their classrooms. Teachers helped young children pack up book bags and put coats on, and then encouraged one final bathroom trip. Some students had to call home with changes in plans, and there was the usual office chaos as a steady stream of parents came in to pick up children once they heard about the early dismissal. Older students prepared for the end of the day with assignments recorded, lockers visited, and backpacks loaded. Teachers gave final reminders, erased boards, and got their teacher bags of work for home packed and ready to leave themselves after a busy week. The kindergarteners were first to head outside to the buses, and shortly after they exited the building, the bell rang to dismiss all students. The hallways were again filled with happy chatter. Finally, the hectic day ended and school was over for the week.

2.

What Do You Mean They're Coming Back?

Students and staff members noticed the bus parking lot was a bit slippery as they exited the building to go to the buses. Some parents in cars mentioned the front driveway becoming icy, and the car line seemed shorter than usual. Once all eight buses were loaded, drivers carefully drove out on the driveway leading up the slope to US Highway 421. A light mist was falling and temperatures hovered just at freezing. As the first bus reached the highway, traffic in both directions was at a standstill. A tractor trailer truck had jackknifed about a mile west of the school and was now blocking traffic in both directions. Parkway's Assistant Principal directed buses to turn around and return to the bus parking lot. Students were unloaded and headed back to their classrooms. When the last car rider was picked up by the last car in line, the other students waiting for parents were sent back to their classrooms. Teachers, who were about to exit the building themselves, were quite surprised. Word spread throughout the building, "They're coming back!" What in the world was going on? The first children to return to the classrooms were excited to tell their teachers that the buses couldn't get out onto the highway.

The principal made an announcement that neither buses nor cars could arrive or leave at this time and for everyone to stand by for further information. Most thought at that time that it would be a short wait, but the temperatures were falling and the misty rain was beginning to ice every surface it touched. When the jack-knifed truck across the highway was finally cleared, traffic on US 421 began to flow again, very slowly. Chains were put on the buses with help from lots of people, and a second attempt was made to load the buses and leave. The kindergarten and first grade teachers can remember making a human chain with the children as they all held hands to get to the buses safely without falling down. This time the buses, even with chains installed, found the surface of the driveway too slippery to be safe. They again returned to the parking lot. Some buses tried a third time to make the trip. At that point it was decided that the buses would not run at all. Everyone at Parkway was officially stuck at school!

At the front of the building some parents who had managed to get to the school to pick up their children were able to leave before conditions became too treacherous. Many cars struggled as tires spun trying to get up the hill to the front entrance. When it became too dangerous to enter the school driveway, a few parents left their cars parked on US 421 and walked very carefully down the sloping driveway and up the parking area to the school to get their children. One parent relates her experience driving on the Blue Ridge Parkway, which was becoming covered with ice, parking, and walking across the highway and to the school entrance to get her two sons. She walked with them, struggling over the icy surfaces, back to her father's truck and made the "scariest ride ever" back to their home. Eventually the roads became impossible to navigate, and no parents were able to get to the school.

The temperature continued to hover just below freezing, with ice building up on all roads, parking lots, cars, trees, and power lines. The principal made the next announcement that all students and staff would be remaining at school indefinitely and for everyone to stay tuned for directions and updates. There was a myriad of responses to this news from both students and staff. Some of the younger children were teary and scared and needed comfort from an adult. Many older students saw it as a chance to socialize with their friends and have an adventure. The adults in the building were most concerned about how to best take care of the students – how to comfort, entertain, feed, and supervise them through the coming hours. When the principal called for all members of the Crisis Team to come to the office, the staff knew answers would be coming soon.

3.

The Crisis Team

Every school in Watauga County had a group of staff members carefully chosen to be on the Crisis Team. This team was a group of representative staff members whose job involved making necessary plans and decisions in an emergency situation at the school. The team members had skills and talents, knowledge and training that could quickly assess an emergency situation and then plan for safety and solutions. They were individuals who could keep a cool head in an emergency and could also keep everyone else calm. Some had training in first aid and CPR, others had knowledge of the layout of the building, and administrators had information about communication, community resources, and recommended procedures from law enforcement and emergency responders. As the members of the team gathered in the office conference room, all had confidence that students and staff would be safe and in good hands.

This group would determine the answers to many questions throughout the afternoon and evening of January 26. They developed a plan for how to communicate with parents, the Watauga County Schools Central Office, and the media. A schedule was created by the team for feeding everyone and for allowing the students to participate in physical activity in the gym, time in the media center, and a session in the computer lab. The team even set up a way for all homeroom teachers to get some much needed relief by circulating the non-homeroom teachers through these classrooms. A telephone system was set up so that any children who wanted to call home could. The information and planning was shared with the entire staff and students through intercom announcements and runners who would come to get classes for the supper meal or for activity time in the gym. The Crisis Team, as the evening got longer and longer, even started contingency planning if the students and staff were to have to spend the night. Sleeping arrangements, local sources of blankets and pillows, more food planning, communicating with parents and the media, and many other details were addressed and put on a shelf in case they were needed.

Each homeroom probably had one half to two thirds of the students they normally had after some students were picked up by parents. The dilemma for teachers, depending on the age of the students, was how to handle this very unusual time. The Crisis Team helped with suggestions. Members of the team gave ideas for students who were having a difficult time and even sat with individual children who were upset. The members of this team provided structure and support all afternoon and evening, freeing classroom teachers to deal with each individual student and his/her needs.

4.

Afternoon Becomes Evening

Young children and older adolescents reacted differently to the predicament of being "stuck at school." For kindergarten-second grade children, staff members initially were comforting a few crying children who didn't understand where their parents were or why they were not going home-or they understood but just weren't happy. This was especially true as darkness descended outside. Students in intermediate and middle grades tended to think of the experience as a party! For all ages, talented, creative, and caring staff members were able to plan activities that would interest and comfort all children and keep them busy and happy. Teachers did not want this time to feel like a regular school day, so no assignments were given. Some children chose to read during the evening. Younger children played dress-up or drew pictures in the art center. They built with blocks and put together puzzles. Other students played games like *Yahtzee* or *Checkers*, *Chess* or *Balderdash*. Many chose to spend the time socializing with friends or listening to music, and this was one of the benefits of the evening – children spent time getting to know students they had not known very well before, for lots of reasons. Many movies were shown across all grade levels, and it was fun to laugh and share those with teachers and friends. Some classrooms had movement games like "Duck, Duck, Goose" or "Who's Got the Bone" to keep children busy and engaged. Some of the older siblings wanted to visit their younger brothers and sisters in the school, and it was heartwarming to see this caring side of students. All over the building, staff and students guided their actions by asking, "What is needed? What would make this situation better? How can I lessen the stress and add to the joy? How can we make sure this is a happy memory?"

Hunger was a pretty obvious issue early in the afternoon, as most children head for the refrigerator when they get home from school each day. Many teachers kept a "snack stash" in their classrooms for occasions when a student might need food or enjoy a treat, so those supplies were quickly depleted as all staff shared what they had. Solving the hunger issue was one of the pressing problems the Crisis Team tackled. Two cafeteria workers – the manager and one of her staff – decided they needed to return to school to help feed everyone. They had already gotten home, but lived close by – within a mile. When they heard on the radio that the students and staff were still at school, they trekked back to the school through the treacherous icy conditions, and got busy in the kitchen. Many staff members helped them prepare chicken sandwiches and pizza. This was the third meal the cafeteria staff had prepared that day! An assembly line of teachers, administrators, custodians, and others formed to fill plates as students came through the line. Classes came to the cafeteria when called and took their food back to the classroom to eat with their friends. Each class experienced a sense of family as they ate and talked together during this shared meal. This family dining atmosphere contributed to the feeling of well-being and safety that prevailed across the school.

None of the people in classrooms and hallways likely ever realized the busy, noisy confusion that was happening in the Parkway School office during this time. The phones never stopped ringing and often many lines were lit up simultaneously. Parents, Central Office personnel, and the media kept the two secretaries swamped most of the afternoon and evening. This took some skill to handle each call professionally, as parents were genuinely concerned about their children. There were a few parents who were somehow able to arrive at the school to pick up children, and the office staff then had to summon the students being picked up to the office over the intercom. Since many children were visiting in classrooms other than their own, the office staff finally gave up calling individual classrooms and just did all-calls that went out across the school. The principal and assistant principal handled many phone calls, continually checked on weather conditions, talked to the media, met with the Crisis Team, and checked on classrooms occasionally to make sure all were fine. WATA 1450 AM, the local radio station in Boone, became Parkway's communication vehicle out to the community. As the station received updates from the school office, the radio staff would broadcast updates to assure all parents that children were in good hands and the situation was under control.

All staff members who did not have homeroom responsibilities helped out in a myriad of ways - relief for classroom teachers, help in the gym, assistance in the cafeteria, leading children to phones, answering phones, helping out in the office, and so much more. A few students had medical issues that needed attention, including one student that had a seizure. All pulled together to do what had to be done. There was no complaining, no gloominess, no disagreement. Teamwork and problem-solving skills were on display across the building, creating positive examples for all students. The entire staff had but one focus – keeping children safe and happy in a stressful situation.

In 1996, no one had a cell phone – that's one reason there are no photos to document this event. Every classroom had a phone, but there were only 4-5 phone lines into the school, and they were kept busy all evening. Students who wanted or needed to call their parents were taken in small groups to one of the phone lines in the building to call and hear their parents' voices and tell them they were OK. Staff members were able to communicate with their families and some parents by email at their computers.

All in all, the evening was a huge success! The atmosphere throughout the school was upbeat – much like it would be on the day of a holiday party. There was an unspoken feeling that everyone at Parkway was a part of something pretty special. Each time the intercom called another student to the office to go home, the student whose name was called would say, "Oh, no! I want to stay!" It felt like leaving the party early - a good sign that the situation was handled well.

5.

The Longest Day Finally Ends

Throughout the evening of January 26 the temperatures outside slowly began to rise, instead of drop as many had feared. Parents had been informed earlier by radio and phone calls that the buses would not run, so they all needed to get to the school to pick up their children when it was safe. One after another, names were called from the intercom that parents had arrived to get their children. Each one hated to leave the group, even the ones who had initially been upset, and the numbers in each classroom dwindled throughout the night. By 9:30 p.m., most students had been picked up; however, a few in each class were there until after 10:00. Everyone was exhausted as the adrenaline finally subsided, but all were happy. The Watauga County Schools Superintendent and a few of his staff came by late in the evening to thank staff members for the great job they did handling the situation. They congratulated each one they met with smiles and hugs and handshakes.

One teacher assistant's husband and son were able to hike to the school by the end of the evening. They went to each staff member, got his/her car keys, and started the car, defrost/heater, and windshield wipers so that each person entered a warm car when starting home. A few staff members reported a harrowing drive home as they encountered side roads and driveways that were still very slick. A few asked their spouses to come pick them up, leaving their cars to get another time.

During the experience that has come to be known as 'The Longest Day,' there was no complaining or negativity that was shared or heard. It was, in the principal's words, Parkway's "Finest Hour."

6.

The Story Lives On

Once all students and staff were safely home and rested through the weekend, Parkway's 'Longest Day' was the subject of much conversation for weeks to come. Parents expressed gratitude in many ways. The principal wrote a letter to the editor of the local newspaper, *The Watauga Democrat*, which also published a story about the experience titled, "Winter Continues to Pound the Area." A T-Shirt was designed and ordered for everyone; it said, 'I Survived The Longest Day-January 26, 1996 Parkway Elementary School.' Many still have their shirts today.

As staff members retire from Parkway, they become a part of a monthly lunch group of Parkway Retired Teachers. Many times the topic of 'The Longest Day' comes up. Memories are shared again and again – laughter rings out as the group recalls particular children or incidents that happened that evening. Sharing these memories brings up a warm and happy feeling; it causes all to remember what it's like to be a part of something bigger than themselves. The idea for this account of January 26, 1996, came from the Parkway Retired Teacher lunch group in the spring of 2019. This book is a culmination of many memories and a tribute to those who made the evening such a success.

In the appendices following you will find some special memories of the evening from students and staff members. The photo of the front of the T-Shirt is on the front cover and Acknowledgement page. A list of students by class with photos of their teachers is included. There are photos of the Parkway Staff as well, all copied from the 1995-96 Parkway yearbook. Most of these wonderful people were on duty on 'The Longest Day.' Readers will also see a recent photo of the entrance to Parkway School as it looked in 2019. The article and letters from the newspaper and several photos of the Parkway Retired Teachers complete *The Long, Longer, Longest Day*.

Acknowledgements

The photos of the staff were copied from the 1995-96 Parkway School yearbook, which was loaned to me by Owen Gray, Parkway School Media Specialist, with permission from the present principal of Parkway School, Patty Buckner. The lists of students by class and the photos of the teachers and assistants were also copied from this 1995-96 yearbook. Thanks to Kathy Idol, former Parkway Media Specialist, who kept all of the yearbooks organized in the Media Center and maintained the scrapbooks of each year in the life of the school. This is where the two letters to the editor in *The Watauga Democrat* were found. I appreciate the work of Louise Miller, who was the faculty sponsor for the 1995-96 yearbook.

The Watauga Democrat article, "Winter Continues to Pound Area," by Anna Oakes, was retrieved from the archives and typed by Kayla Lasure.

The photographs of the school driveway and the front of the school were taken by Billie Hicklin using a Samsung Galaxy S8+ Smartphone.

The Parkway School logo on the Parkway School sign was designed by Parkway parent and local artist Richard Tumbleston.

The photographs of the Parkway Retired Teachers were taken with Marsha Fletcher's I-Phone.

Many, many thanks to all students, parents, and staff members who shared their memories to make this account possible. This book is a gift to the Parkway Media Center, where it will hopefully be read by Parkway students and staff – past, present, and future – to keep the story alive. *The Long, Longer, Longest Day* represents all that is good in a group of people who pulled together for a common, worthy, selfless goal. Bravo to this group! May we forever remain **PARKWAY PROUD!**

Appendix I

Special Memories

From the Parkway Retired Lunch Group, parents, students:

Marsha Fletcher remembered that as some parents drove up to get their children, hungry staff members would ask, "Do you have any food?" One parent gave Marsha his leftover dinner from Makoto's Restaurant!

Susan Suddreth shared her memory of the children in her first grade class forming a "human chain" to get to the buses – twice! She also shared that after this event happened, she carried a change of clothes and a pillow in her car during the winter months, just in case! Susan remembers one set of parents telling her that they heard on the radio that the children were safe in the hands of the Parkway Staff, so they went to dinner and a movie!

Susan Chandler related that she had a student whose activity level increased as time went by. This made for an interesting evening, until her husband came by to check on her and taught the active student to play poker! This kept the 4th grader occupied the rest of the evening.

Teresa Lentz remembered that several of her second graders were upset initially when they couldn't leave. Then when their parents came to pick them up they didn't want to leave because they were having so much fun.

Susan Lawrence recalled that her eighth graders were ecstatic at the possibility that this could turn into a mega-sleepover. She and her fellow teachers were hoping not, but pondered how to police their puberty-driven charges through an all-nighter, should it come to pass! She remembers two of her students who wanted to walk home, were told they could not, and then disappeared enroute to the gym. Later one of their mothers arrived to pick them up after sitting in that awful traffic for hours, only to discover they were already at home!

Bain Winkler remembers a set of her kindergarten parents whose child was the last one in her classroom that night. After some time passed she called the parents, who evidently had not been listening to the radio, and they were still waiting on the bus to bring their child home! After being told the buses weren't running, they were there in twenty minutes to pick up the child.

One of Parkway's former teachers (who later returned), **Alice Greer**, had moved to Winston Salem at the time. She and her husband turned on the news the evening of January 26 where it was announced that Parkway School in Watauga County was still at school because of the ice storm that had paralyzed the mountains! She remembered the word "paralyzed" being used by the broadcaster and wished she had been there…she thinks!

Christy Hill, the music teacher, remembers an 8th grade student whose dad made it to the school to pick him up earlier in the afternoon. He didn't want to go, but his teachers urged him to go along with his dad. Christy also remembers that a policy was created that would allow Parkway School to dismiss one half hour earlier than other schools on weather related early dismissal days in the future, especially after this scenario happened a second time.

Billie Hicklin's 7th grade classroom had windows that looked out onto the bus entrance to the back of the building and the bus parking lot. She remembers well the buses leaving that day – the first time – and a sinking feeling when she saw them returning. There was a "What are we in for?" feeling as she projected ahead into the evening. The three seventh grade classrooms divided into a game room, a movie room, and a socializing room. Students could move back and forth from room to room and even gather in groups in the hallway. Billie remembers telling the story of this long day at school to future classes, to friends, and to family over the years.

Stephen Schmal remembers all of his snack stash being consumed in the early hours of the afternoon. He remembers one middle school student who was picked up by his parents, but then walked back to school because he didn't want to miss the fun! Stephen also recalls a student having a seizure during the evening, and he praises his capable colleagues who attended to the student until everything was fine.

Michelle Cox Wall was a student teacher in Mrs. Suddreth's first grade class when 'The Longest Day' occurred. What is so neat is that Michelle was an alumna of Parkway School! Her father, James, was the custodian on duty that evening, and he helped out in many areas, including preparation of dinner! She noticed the different reactions of the first graders – boys who were afraid and girls who treated the event like a slumber party! She remembers thoughts of possibly having to spend the night, as many other staff members silently contemplated. Michelle went on to become a teacher in another part of the state, but she said she still talks about the longest day. She said this day is one of the most memorable days she's ever experienced, "with a blend of stress, surprising fun, and bonding that occurred in a unique situation."

Tammy Stephens had two sons at Parkway that night and she and her father decided to come get them on the icy Blue Ridge Parkway. They left his truck on the side of the road, hiked across the highway to the school, got the boys and went back to the truck. Someone drove along with hay in a trailer, and they spread the hay on the icy highway to help the truck get traction. She said it was a scary ride home!

Then 7th grader **Jessica Woods Ashley** probably exemplified the thoughts of many middle grade students, thinking "... Oh my! I'm going to have to sleep at school? With BOYS? What if I snore? What if the power goes off and we freeze to death? Surely my mom and dad can make it here to get me! Does this mean we don't have to follow the regular school rules? Who am I joking? I'll follow them anyways – Just wait til I tell everybody else about this!"

And finally, **Lauren Wellborn,** a 7th grader, remembers the day well. She recalls a group of friends in the hallway playing board games, particularly *Balderdash*. They all laughed until they cried at the outlandish definitions they made up for the words in the game. She remembers eating lots of cookies, and then getting picked up along with her 8th grade brother, Joe, and being "a little bummed" they didn't get stuck overnight! She says, "That was one of my favorite days ever as a kid. It was so novel and fun, and an opportunity to play with our peers which is less available in 7th grade than in earlier grades. Ya'll (staff) made it really fun. And thanks for putting in that extra effort – I'm sure you were much less excited about being stuck than we were :)."

Appendix II.

Do You Know These 1995-96 Parkway Teachers, Staff and Students?

Mrs. Joan Hampton  and Mrs. Joan Golds  Kindergarten: Jacqueline Audet,
Dustin Baldwin, Darren Cook, Kayla Dollar, Brandon Farthing, Annie Laurie Fuller,
Taylor Greer, J.C. Hicks, Michelle Horton, Bryan Jellerson, Macy Johnson, Cobern
Mahoney, Trinity Molenda, Joy Mulneix, Megan Perry, Shawn **Presnell, Marc Stephens,**
Amber Stradley, Taylor **Tugman, Michael Vollmer,** **Hailey Watson, Orin Wheeler**

Mrs. Peggy Oehm  and Mrs. Jan Roark  **Kindergarten**: Ashlyn Baird,
Nic Callahan, Thomas Ch, Kathy Cook, Danny Edmisten, Mary Margaret Holden, Jamie
Hopkins, Paige Hopkins, Thayer Horton, Thomas Lambert, Davie McGuinn, Chase
McIlwain, Cursty McLean, Jesse Oxentine, Crystal Roark, Andrew Sailors, Daniel Seats,
Ethan Suddreth, Amber Townsend, Brandy Trivette, Benjamin Vollmer, Alliso
Winkler

Mrs. Bain Winkler  and Mrs. Joann Ray  Kindergarten: Adam
Chiarolanzio, Gloria Coffey, Madison Ericksen, Andrew Greene, David
Harmon, Chelsie Harmann, Justin Hyatt, Layla Joes, Matthew Love, Lee Million, Ian Parker,
Casey Parlier, Tony Potter, Roger Smith, Hannah Sofield, Elliot Todd, Kyle Todd, Sarah
Triplett, Samuel Washburn, Garrett Williams, Charlene Winkler

Mrs. Nancy Cooke  and Mrs. Jane Noble  1st Grade: Josh Adkins,
Tierra Berry, Breanna Brown, J. Jay Burchette, Travis Coffey, Jeremy Elliott, Jonathan
Greene, Leah Hamption, Alex Higgins, Tyler Hite, Allison Huffman, Anna Maria
Jacenko, Aaron Jestes, Ashley Jordan, Barrett Joyner, Jason Krontz, Abby Lowder,
Cressandra McCrea, Allison Meggison, Brooke Miller, Brittney Osborne, Michael
Parsons, Heather Pendley, Ashlely Roten, Aaron Shaki, Tina Shook, Brittany Trivette,
Darren Vannoy, Levi Watson, Shane Watson

Mrs. Susan Suddreth  and Mrs. Debbie Teague  1st Grade:
Ryan Anderson, Nikki Biggers, Victoria Buckley, Jessica Butler, Seth Cook, William
DeJonge, Christoper Eller, Lindsey Gantt, Catherine Graybeal, Caleb Green, Colt
Greer, Joseph Greer, Amanda Hampton, Sarah Marsh, Sarah McCullough, Ellen
McLean, Lindsey Messenkopf, Dillon Millaway, Matthew Moretz, Erica Oxentine,
Creston Triplett, Caleb Trivette, Landon Wallace, Grady Watson, Jason Watson, Revecca
Watson, Kelly Willis

Mrs. Temple Jones  **2nd –Grade:** Amy Cole, Jordan Cook, Caroline Crom, Jacob Dockery, Adam Edwards, Griffin Eriksen, Kyle Greene, Laura Hackney, Leslie Hardy, Cari Joseph, Morgan Lawrence, Jeffrey Lunsford, Andrew Mackorell, Rebecca Meier, Daniel Michael, Sierena Miller, Jonathan Pope, CJ Reed, Nicole Seats, Michael Steele, Craig Stuber, Daniel Wallace, Brook Warren

Mrs. Teresa Lentz  **and Mrs. Linda Simcox**  **2nd Grade:** Ashley Allegro, Paul Baldwin, Aidan Brewer, Jennifer Callahan, Dustin Carlton, Cory Coffey, Marcus Cornett, Paige Daganhardt, Jessie Davis, Tara Fickling Ashley Greene, Thomas Holden, Gus Johnson, Lane Johnson, Molly Johnson, Sarah Johnson, Holt Mikeal, Charity Miller, Walker Moseley, Alicia Peele, Amanda Reed, Ashley Shook, Patrick Vollmer, Kelly Walsh, David Winkler

Mrs. Kathy McCreary  **and Mrs. Suzanne Jordan**  **2nd Grade:** Hannah Cameron, Richard Campbell, Meg Cook, Patrick Fuller, Kelly Greene, Anna Gustaveson, Shauntrelle Horton, Tracy Lentz, Jennifer Lockhart, Josh McMillan, Sydeena Miller, Eric Moretz, Joey Parsons, Johnathan Pleasant, Annette Ploszaj, Eric Rader, Jacob Ray, Kayla Ruppard, Justin Sailors, Michael Simpkins, Michael Smith, Casey Ward, Melissa Ward, Gabriel Williams, Khrista Winkler

Mrs. Beth Carrin  **and Mrs. Chris Miller**  **3rd Grade:** Eden Auton, Chris Baird, Megan Bradford, Jordan Brown, Robert Chiarolanzio, Crystal Coffey, Kiesha Congelosi, Brian Cook, Elizabeth Culatta, Bradley Farthing, Dylan Fuller, Cierra Greene, Trathen Greene, Nicklas Greer, Josh Hamby, Payne Joyner, Matthew Lebert, Callie Lewis, Lauren Maltba, Travis Saltares, Miranda Seats, Luke Short, Ben Style, Anna Tugman, Felicia Ward, Wesley Ward

Mrs. Marie Graham  **and Mrs. Bonnie Steelman**  **3rd Grade:** Desiree Aparicio, Brittany Beach, Uland Bradford, Ginny Buckley, Brandon Carlton, Joshua Carroll, Caity Carter, Brian Clevenger, Corey Edmisten, Tracy Fee, Tara Gaskill, Shane Greene, Jordan Horton, Jennifer Maltba, Tommy McKiernan, Amber Moore, Paige Moretz, Crystal Newman, Sally Parlier, Angie Roark, Kelly Scroggs, Brett Stephens, Josh Tester, Sarah Washburn, Cody Watson

Ms. Mardy Brown  **4th Grade:** Stacy Campany, Nathan Campbell, Sara Cole, Stephanie Crissman, Carlee Critcher, Mindy Culler, Jenna Curry, Kristi Gragg, Josh Hampton, Meghan Harris, John Holden, Matthew Huskins, Kevin Jellerson, Anthony Jestes, Renn Johnson, Wesley Lincoln, Timothy Love, Amber Moretz, Mason Moseley, Kenneth Roark, Terra Roberts, Francois Schneyder, Ramsey Tilson

Mrs. Patti Hensley  **4th Grade:** Samuel Addison, Chad Audet, Terran Berry, Joey Butler, Tracy Callahan, Grace Coffey, Aaron Daganhardt, Kevin Dreibelbis, Chris Eggers, Paul Eldridge, Jama Greene, Tylor Greene, Thomas Lunsford, Candace Miller, Megan Moretz, April Morris, Gabriel Pagan, Kelly Scott, Natalie Vannoy, Jessi Wagoner, Mary Katherine Willis, Whitney Wineberg, Holly Winkler

Mr. Tom Van Gilder  **4th Grade:** Marcus Anderson, McKenzie Anderson, Ross Forman, Autumn Greene, Jack Hackney, Alicia Hampton, Heather Hawley, Jessica Haywood, Eric Hicks, Joe Hicks, Dustin Kerley, Jonathan Matar, Ivy Mauney, Trevor McCrea, Matt McIlwain, Nathan Meier, Steven Midkiff, Carson Oxentine, Aaron Peele, Cara Ray, Angela Shook, Amber Smith, Matthew Smith, Jeremy Watson, Brittany Wiesz, Jessica Wineberg

Mrs. Joanie Foster  **5th Grade:** McKenna Anderson, Katie Baker, Jimmy Batchelor, Stacey Cearley, Arielle Church, Victor Ellison, Lana Greene, Tracy Johnson, Shae Jones, Jeffrey Jordan, John Jordan, Chris Mahoney, Elijah Mulneix, Jessica Pace, Michael Pope, Patrick Ray, Josh Spiceland, Ryan Sprader, Heather Stidham, Emily Styers, Ben Teague

Mrs. Lou Moore  **5th Grade:** Kimberly Blanchard, Ashley Bradford, Ben Caviness, Scott Dunn, Michael Eller, Michael Garner, Brandy Greene, Kyle Greene, Ryan Hampton, Willie Hicks, Stephen Holder, Beth Johnson, Joseph Love, Lydia Miller, Heather Ray, James Shore, Ashley Suddreth, Gaylin Swibold, Christopher Trivette, Matthew Washburn

Mrs. Betsy Morris  **5th Grade:** Melanie Barwick, Kalyn Bates, Alan Byerly, Bradley Carlton, Teddy Clevenger, Michelle Cook, Danielle Hampton, Sheena Honeycutt, Alicia Kuntzman, Haley Lyons, Adam Randall, Patrick Saunders, Lauren Sumrell, Stacy Swift, Bobby Taylor, Jessica Todd, Jordan Todd, Gary Watson, Meade Willis, Matthew Winkler

Mrs. Carolyn Eggers  **6th Grade:** Cody Allegro, Brad Butler, Sarah Davis, Bronson Ericksen, Chris Farthing, Ginny Farthing, Matt Fowler, Joseph Garner, Cindy Gragg, Adam Greene, Emily Haibach, Candice Hamby, Staci Hodges, Chris Joyner, Mandy Lebert, Jamie McElyea, Andi Miller, Michael Peek, Mark Pennell, Georgia Ray, Carolyn Reynolds, Willie Roberts, Kim Sacco, Rachel Spiceland, Andrew Trivette, Dale Trivette, Alisha Woodall

Mrs. Connie Goff  **6th Grade:** Jason Brown, Amanda Chestnut, Justin Cole, Crystal Culler, Allison Dillard, Danyale Elliott, Carrie Graybeal, Randi Green, Jessica Hampton, Chad Higgins, Natalie Jones, Heather Kerley, Emmet Lunsford, Joshua Moore, Gregory Moretz, Jonathan Newsome, Samantha Newton, Jesse Optekar, Pamela Penuel, Tonya Pope, Jacob Shook, April Stradley, Frankie Taylor, Keri Triplett, John Tumbleston, Danielle Tyson, Dustin Vannoy, Thomas Wise

Mr. Stephen Schmal  **6th Grade:** Christopher Auton, Rori Brewer, Eric Brown, Matthew Carter, Kim Clontz, Sheldon Coffey, David Frissell, Kacy Goff, Emily Harris, Beckett Hills, Micah Johnson, Rebecca King, Tara Lentz, Tommy Love, Morgan McCreary, Eric Midkiff, Samantha Moretz, Ricky Osborne, Matthew Reece, Kolette Schneyder, Meagan Schreiber, Josh Smith, Orin Smith, Kristin Stroupe, Amanda Tester, Candis Watson, Dustin Watson

Mrs. Billie Hicklin  **7th Grade:** Danae Addison, Karisa Aparicio, Eddie Birdwell, Patrick Callahan, Holly Chamra, Joni Christenbury, Luke Critcher, Alicia Greene, Shaun Greene, Greg Harmon, Katie Holder, Melissa Howard, James Hyatt, Estrella Jordan, Jamie McGuinn, Jonathan Miller, Bess Nelson, Leslie O'Loughlin, Adam Rawls, Bryan Sherbet, Daniel Whitson, Janell Wright

Ms. Crystal McNamee  **7th Grade:** Morgan Anderson, Kerri Andrews, Melissa Atwood, Jason Carlton, Aaron Coffey, Kenny Curry, Tony Del Sarto, James Fickling, Brad Greene, Randy Greene, Kelly Hartmann, Steven Horton, Brittney Miler, Tami Nicholls, Jarhett Norris, Laura Russel, Steven Sacco, Amber Smith, Charles Style, Shelley Watson, Lauren Wellborn, Jessica Wood

Mr. Gene Moore  **7th Grade:** Paige Abbott, Nathan Bland, Jessica Cook, David Culver, Shayla Dodgge, Adam Greer, Susan Hamby, Amy Hawks, Emily Isaacs, Jenny Jacobs, Luke Linclon, David Matar, Joey McKiernan, Will Mulneis, Kelly Murphy, Wesley Nelson, Racheal Rellea, Tracie Triplett, Blake Van Brouwer, Andrew Wallace, Phillip Watson, Crystal Winkler, Kari Wright

Mrs. Susan Lawrence, Mrs. Mary Jo Pritchard, Mrs. Margaret Weaver 8th Grade: Tyson Abbott, Matt Anderson, Nicole Ashley, Cindy Barlow, Laurel Bates, Kirsten Brewer, Stephanie Caltrider, Laura Caviness, Jacob Chaney, Katie Christenbury, Adam Cole, Nathan Cook, Katie Cooper, Jeremy Cox, Justin Critcher, Brandon Dollar, Dusty Dreibelbis, Jennny Dubberly, Ashley Eldridge, Daniel Eller, Kevin Eller, Jimmy Elliott, Noah Gordon, Jason Greene, Justin Greene, Kim Greene, Wayne    Greene, Steve Hampton, Lisa Harmon, David Harris, Ben Hicks, Doyle Hicks, Robert Higgins, Travis Hodges, Jennifer Holman, Josh Honeycutt, Steven Hopper, Ananda Janowiak, Phillip Johnson, Leslie Jones, Sarah King, Beth Lethco, Aaron Lincoln, Kristan Meister, Seth Miller, Tara Moore, Justin Moretz, Shane Moretz, Andy Natusch, Caleb Newton, Dustin Nicholls, Joel Osborne, Trae Pace, Matt Potter, Shelly Radar, Leah Russell, Kristan Sacco, Crissy Sanders, Kristi Scroggs,

Justin Short, Logan Sumrell, John Taylor, Leanna Terrell, Raynette Tester, Marshall Thomas, Barney Van Devender, Andy Waters, Carrie Waters, Johnathan Watson, Joe Wellborn, Molly Whitson, John Worley

Faculty and Staff

Gary Childers
Principal

Merle Todd
Vice Principal

Gail Norman
Secretary

Donna Gragg
Secretary

Kathy Idol
Media Specialist

Aretta Caroll
Media Assistant

Nancy DeLargy
Spanish

Eve Whitlock
Mathematics

Marsh Fletcher
Technology

Sally Whitson
Physical Education

Robert McKethan
Physical Education

Faculty and Staff

Barbara Pinnix
Cafeteria Manager

Theresa Burchette
Cafeteria Staff

Loretta Cornejo
Cafeteria Staff

Velma Greene
Cafeteria Staff

Zola Idol
Cafeteria Staff

Mary Henson
Reading

Susan Wilson
Resource

Judy Greene
Reading

Carolyn Pope
Counselor

Sandra Smith
Counselor

Linda Craig
Counselor

Louise Miller
Enrichment

Faculty and Staff

Buck Roberts
Band and Orchestra

Christy Hill
Chorus and Music

Virginia Gable
Vocation

Bob Meier
Vocation

James Cox
Custodian

Mark Claybrook
Custodian

Virginia Watson
Custodian

Bus Drivers
(L-R) Deborah Lawrence, Zola Idol, Darlene Caudill, Ann Hamby, Virginia Watson, Janice Miller, James Early, Allen Jestes, Doug Moore. Not pictured: Cindy Jones

Appendix III.

This story ran in the January 29, 1996 edition of the **Watauga Democrat**.
"Winter Continues to Pound Area."

Five motor vehicle accidents due to ice and freezing rain on U.S. 421 east rendered traffic and more than 600 students and staff at Parkway Elementary School immobile Friday. Icing conditions were reported by the N.C. State Highway Patrol and N.C. Department of Transportation. The highway patrol reported 26 accidents throughout the county that day.

Five patients were transported to Watauga Medical Center to be treated and released, said Jerry Moretz of Watauga Medical Center.

However, Merle Todd, Parkway Assistant Principal, said buses could not have run even if driving conditions had been safe. "When we were ready to dismiss students (on Friday), traffic was not moving on 421," he said.

As a result, a message was sent out on the airways for parents to come pick up their children. Two more unsuccessful attempts were made to run buses throughout the afternoon.

Todd said the last child was picked up after 10 p.m. Friday. One or two children were delivered home by Parkway staff.

Seven of the nine Watauga County Schools were successfully dismissed early at 1:45 p.m. Friday with few complications, since the storm was isolated to southern and eastern sectors of the county, said Don Lucas, supervisor of elementary education for Watauga County. Blowing Rock Elementary was the only other school without buses running, based on reports from Blowing Rock Police and bus drivers throughout the area, according to Principal Gary Cone. Cone said a majority of the parents normally pick up children at Blowing Rock Elementary. Teachers directly telephoned parents whose children ride buses and a message was broadcast on the radio station.

Lucas said Watauga County Schools have seen an unusual number at this time of year for missed days, delays and early dismissals due to weather. Watauga County built 12 additional days into the school year, in case of weather. So far, they have missed 10 days.

Anna Oakes *Editor, Watauga Democrat & All About Women* Mountain Times Publications 474 Industrial Park Drive, Boone, NC 28607 828-278-3601

Appendix IV.

Letters to the Editor – Watauga Democrat – January, 1996

Parkway School

As parents of a kindergarten child at Parkway Elementary School, we would like to express our deep appreciation to everyone there for the excellent way the situation was handled this past Friday when the buses were not allowed to run due to ice.

We are so thankful that every consideration was made for the safety and well-being of the children.

Even though it was certainly a very tiring and difficult time for the teachers and staff, we still saw smiles and happy children as well as adults when we were finally able to get there to pick up our daughter about 8:15 p.m.

We would like to say a special "thank you" to Peggy Oehm and Jan Roarke for keeping our child safe, happy, and feeling secure.

We would also like to thank WATA radio for its excellent coverage of the situation. They kept parents very informed as to what our children were doing and kept reminding us that the children were safe and in the best of care.

Thank you to everyone involved in bringing about a happy end to this difficult situation.

ROGER and KAREN BAIRD
Boone

Parkway proud

Friday, Jan. 26, will be a day and evening forever implanted in the memory of all Parkway School family members.

Who would have known when we began the day that a sudden freezing rain would cause most of us to still be at school until around 9:30 that evening.

In the 24 years I've had the privilege to work in the schools of Watauga County, this was without doubt one of the most challenging, yet gratifying, days of my career.

Challenges were successfully met by faculty, staff, students, parents, administrators and volunteers throughout the evening.

To list all the needs which had to be met and how they were handled by everyone would take a feature article. Suffice it to say, it was a monumental effort.

What I would like to focus on is the gratification many others and I have felt from having gone through this experience. I was deeply moved by the response of everyone during this event.

During the entire time we were involved, the faculty's and staff's focus was on what needed to be done to provide for the needs of our students.

Even though the bodies were beginning to tire, the attitudes remained positive.

Our parents were supportive of the decisions which were made and have expressed their appreciation in many ways for the care we provided their children.

I would be remiss not to reflect on the response of the children. They were terrific!

With just a small number of exceptions, they seemed to understand the situation we were in and the need to make the best of it. (As a matter of fact, we had many who wanted to stay longer!)

As I've been asked to reflect on the events of the day and how we dealt with them, the term heroic has consistently seemed the appropriate word to describe my view of the actions of the people who were here.

I want to follow that by taking the opportunity to express my thanks to the faculty, staff, students, and parents for what they did Friday, Jan. 26, 1996, and for what they do every other day of the school year. It's gratifying to be a part of such a school and community.

Remaining Parkway Proud!
GARY L. CHILDERS
Principal

Appendix V.

Parkway School in 2019

Appendix VI.

Parkway Retired Teachers

Left to Right: Cinda McGuinn, Bernie Edwards, Steve Idol, Sondra Edwards, Pam Meyer, Mike Fletcher, Emily and Gary Childers, Karen Crotts, Pam Todd, Donna Gragg, Merle Todd, Billie Hicklin, Vicki Unmack, Marsha Fletcher, Kathy Idol, Bain Winkler, Joan Hampton, Seated: Charles and Barbara McDaniel, Judy Greene

Front left to back around table:

Emily Childers, Sue Ward, Deane Shuford, Joan Hampton, Sondra Edwards, Kathy Idol, Billie Hicklin, Donna Gragg, Judy Greene, Marsha Fletcher, Linda Craig, Gary Childers

Left to right: Natalie Willis, Joanie Foster, David Davis, Sondra Edwards, Linda Craig, Merle Todd, Karen Crotts, Pam Meyer, Marsha Fletcher, Vicki Unmack, Joan Hampton, Judy Greene, Gary Childers, Beth Carrin, Teresa Lentz, Louise Miller, Kathy Idol

Afterword

The Long, Longer, Longest Day is written based on the memories of people who were really there when Parkway School students and staff were not able to get home on that fateful day in 1996. Some memories are sharp and some have faded, but they are shared as best remembered. There was a second day a year later when a sudden snow storm dumped many inches quickly in the early afternoon, and Parkway Students and staff were again stranded at school. Some who were asked to share their recollections said they couldn't remember if their memories were from the first or second time that students and staff had to remain at school into the night. This story is probably a combination of memories from both days, and many of the procedures, decisions, and activities were most likely the same. On both days, it was a special memory for all.

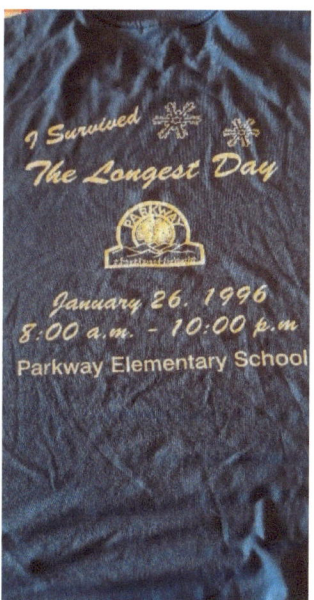

www.ingramcontent.com/pod-product-compliance
Lightning Source LLC
Chambersburg PA
CBHW041543040426
42446CB00003B/216